# DAYTON ★ AIR ★ SHOW

# DAYTON ★ AIR ★ SHOW
## a photographic celebration

Photos by Ty Greenlees
Text by Timothy R. Gaffney

ORANGE FRAZER PRESS
Wilmington, Ohio

ISBN-13: 978-1-933197-45-6
ISBN-10: 1-933197-45-5

Additional copies of *Dayton Air Show: A Photographic Celebration* may be ordered directly from:

Orange Frazer Press
P.O. Box 214
Wilmington, OH 45177

Telephone 1.800.852.9332 for price and shipping information.
Website: www.orangefrazer.com

Photography: Ty Greenlees
Text: Timothy R. Gaffney
Design: Chad DeBoard

Library of Congress Cataloging-in-Publication Data

Greenlees, Ty, 1966-
   The Dayton Air Show : a photographic celebration / photos by Ty Greenlees ; text By Timothy R. Gaffney.
      p. cm.
   ISBN-13: 978-1-933197-45-6 (alk. paper)
   ISBN-10: 1-933197-45-5
   1.  Dayton Air Show (Dayton, Ohio)--History--Pictorial works. 2.  Air shows--Ohio--Dayton Metropolitain Area--History--Pictorial works. 3. Stunt flying--Ohio--Dayton Metropolitain Area--History--Pictorial works. I. Gaffney, Timothy R. II. Title.
   TL506.U6D3847 2008
   797.5'4--dc22
                              2008007200

Printed in China

# DEDICATION

We dedicate this book to the air show pilots who gave their all to turn our eyes skyward and let our imaginations take wing.

# TABLE OF CONTENTS

# ACKNOWLEDGEMENTS

We did not set out, back in 1985, to produce a book about the Dayton Air Show. Our only goals were to produce good stories and pictures for our newspaper, the *Dayton Daily News*, and to indulge our mutual passion for aviation. Our work depended on supportive editors, cooperative sources, helpful volunteers and loving families. Consequently, so did this book. More people than we can list here helped us in large or small ways over the years. Sean D. Tucker has been a news source, mentor and friend for most of the years we covered the show. Many of the best pictures in this book would not have been possible without the expert help of Sean's announcer and photo chase pilot, Brian Norris. Patty Wagstaff has been a constant friend and mentor about the air show business. Mike Emoff, chairman of the air show board, and past chairman Don Kinlin helped in many ways, as did Terry Grevious, executive director; Brenda Kerfoot, general manager; former Executive Director Chuck Newcomb and his Communications Director Kim Dell; former air show president Henry Ogrodzinski; former Air Operations Director Clair Potter, and the late George W. "J.R." Wedekind Jr., former executive director. Skip Peterson, retired *Dayton Daily News* chief photographer, showed us the ropes and mentored us in many ways when we began covering the air show. Many volunteers helped us over the years and continue to do so, especially Sheila Wallace and John McCance. Ty Greenlees is especially grateful for the support of his wife Amy Hale, his parents Jim and Daisy Greenlees, and Jerry and Alice Braun, his uncle and aunt in Fairborn, who supported his airplane fascination before he could. Tim Gaffney will always be grateful to Grant Jackson, who as assistant metro editor supported his request for the newspaper to authorize—and pay for—a ten-minute, $3,500 flight in a Soviet MiG-29 fighter; to Jim Ripley, who supported it as metro editor, and to the late Max Jennings, who approved it as editor and later made it his favorite tale of editorial extravagance. Finally, we wish to acknowledge Marcy Hawley, publisher of Orange Frazer Press, for seeing merit in our proposal, and graphic designer Chad DeBoard, for raising it to a new level.

#  FOREWORD

Someone once described air shows as the Indianapolis 500, Top Gun and the Fourth of July all rolled into one. ★ As a pilot who has dedicated his entire adult life to the art form of aerobatic flight, I have to say it is much more than that. For the pilots, event organizers, dedicated volunteers and most important, the spectators, air shows represent everything that is so very special about America. ★ Passion is the fuel for all of us involved in this very unique industry. Our goal through flight is to inspire people to dream, educate them so that they can realize those dreams and share in the thrill of dreams accomplished. ★ It is such a delicious feeling diving into the air show arena at full throttle, one mile above the earth. All of your senses are alive. There is only the present. The wings become my arms and I feel every nuance of the aircraft. The earth and sky melt together into one kaleidoscope of colors as I begin tumbling, twirling, twisting, spinning and cartwheeling through the sky. I feel at home, I'm one with my flying machine and in complete control, in search of the perfect flight. ★ It is my desire to have the audience viscerally feel the power of the Skydance. I invite them to live vicariously through me and share with them the incredible magic of flight. ★ Without the support of the community, the diligence of the event organizers and the passion of the hundreds and hundreds of volunteers, I would not have a stage upon which to perform. Also, the spectator would not have the opportunity to clutch their child's hand and say, "You can fly, too!" They are the true heroes of the air show industry. ★ The Vectren Dayton Air Show Presented by Kroger has an incredibly rich and prestigious history. For me, it has always been a huge honor to be invited to perform at the home of Orville and Wilbur Wright. To be flying in the same arena, over the same ground where the greatest aviators in the world have flown, is a dream come true. ★ Live your passion and let it be your fuel to push your dreams where they have never been before.

God Bless America!

*Sean D. Tucker*

Sean D. Tucker

"Dayton means air show" has been a popular promotional pitch for the Dayton Air Show. Given Dayton's role in the invention of the airplane, and the air show industry that has grown up around it, the reverse could also be said—in many ways, air show means Dayton.

Any air show, anywhere, owes a nod of thanks to the Wright brothers. Wilbur and Orville Wright invented the airplane in their West Dayton bicycle shop and tested it on North Carolina's Outer Banks. After four powered flights at Kitty Hawk on December 17, 1903, they returned to Dayton to continue their flying experiments on Huffman Prairie in Greene County. Their first semi-public flights took place there in 1904 and 1905. They weren't air shows, but interested neighbors, passengers on a nearby rail line, and some members of the local press witnessed their history-making flights.

In 1908, the Wrights stunned the world with nearly simultaneous exhibition flights on both sides of the Atlantic. Wilbur electrified Europe at Le Mans with flights beginning on August 8, and Orville followed on September 3 at Fort Myer, Virginia.

The Wright brothers' exhibitions showed the age of practical flight had arrived. It was an age that advanced rapidly, spurred by international air meets that offered big cash prizes for new records in distance, speed and altitude. The air meets were wildly popular. The 1909 meet in Reims, France, was said to have drawn between 300,000 and 500,000 people; North America's first great meet, at Dominguez Field near Los Angeles in January 1910, drew a crowd estimated at upwards of a quarter-million. Aerial performers, who had thrilled crowds with daredevil acts in balloons and airships, quickly seized on the nimbler airplane for more dramatic stunts.

In 1909 and 1910, the Wrights had their hands full forming their airplane company, setting up production, and defending their patent. But competitors were exhibiting their products to win cash prizes and promote sales. Wilbur and Orville formed the Wright Company exhibition team in January 1910. Orville trained most of the pilots at the company's new flying school on Huffman Prairie.

Their foray into the embryonic air show business was troubled and brief. The conservative Wrights frowned on stunts, but exhibition pilots were a young, fearless lot, and safety standards had yet to be developed. The pilots didn't even wear seatbelts as they pushed the limits of their machines and their own skills. Two Wright team pilots died in crashes before the year was out, and the brothers dissolved the team in November 1911. But Wright exhibition pilots were among the airmen who gave many Americans their first glimpse of the new age of flight.

Barnstormers entertained rural crowds after World War I. Air racing flourished in the 1920s. Major events enjoyed support from the armed forces, which continue to value the air show as a venue for showcasing U.S. air power, promoting public support, and recruiting new members.

The course of history would give Dayton's air shows a distinctly military flavor.

World War I and local political clout made Dayton a national center for military aviation technology, training, and logistics. In 1917, the Army established Fairfield Air Depot and Wilbur Wright Field in Greene County, on land that included Huffman Prairie. It established McCook Field just north of downtown Dayton as its technology center. McCook's engineers invented the freefall parachute and broke new ground in the fields of aerial reconnaissance, armament, high-altitude flight and radio navigation, to name but a few. (In a convoluted consolidation, McCook was closed in 1927 and its missions moved to the new Wright Field; Fairfield and Wilbur Wright became Patterson Field, and Patterson and Wright formed today's Wright-Patterson Air Force Base. Huffman Prairie is preserved as a National Park site on the base.)

Military commanders and Dayton civic leaders pro-moted the bases to local citizens and the world at large. The McCook Field Air Carnival of 1923 drew an estimated 90,000 paying guests, with perhaps three times that many watching from outside the gates. Aerial fare for the Labor Day event included mock dogfights, parachute jumps, stunt flying and balloon rides.

Wilbur Wright Field hosted the fifth International Air Races from October 2-4, 1924. Just twenty years after the Wright brothers' first flights on Huffman Prairie, thousands of people—Orville Wright among them—flocked to the field, aided by roads widened for the event. They found "exhibits to stare at, races to gasp at, 'stunts' to make one marvel," *Time* reported in its October 13 edition. While no European nation competed, the races drew many of America's best-known aviators—some already based at McCook. The prestigious Pulitzer Trophy race—the event's grand finalé—was marred by the death of Army Capt. Burt Skeel, whose plane came apart as he made a diving run at the starting line.

Times were different then. In the publicity campaign for the 1924 air races, McCook pilots leafleted nearby towns at night. To make sure people noticed, they set off strings of small signal bombs towed behind their planes. In her book *McCook Field 1917-1927: The Force Behind America's Golden Age of Flight*, Mary Ann Johnson writes that one bomb broke loose over Richmond, Indiana. The bomb didn't explode, but it went through a house roof; the homeowner billed the government ten dollars. A Fairfield Air Depot pamphlet of May 25, 1929, described an upcoming Air Corps demonstration that was to include 100 airplanes making machine-gun and bomb attacks on dummy ground targets. Advised the pamphlet, "As live ammunition and fragmentation bombs will be used, spectators are cautioned to remain behind the ropes."

Apparently the biggest military show ever around Dayton was Wright Field's Armed Forces Fair in October 1945. Wright Field was the Army's center for aeronautical research, development, and intelligence. Base history records say more than a million people from the U.S. and 26 foreign countries swarmed the base for a week to gawk at previously secret German and Japanese hardware that had been captured and taken there for analysis.

A May open house became an annual tradition at Wright-Patterson. In 1950, it became an all-services event. Mock air and ground assaults, low-altitude aerial refueling demonstrations and sonic booms were typical attractions.

Big shows weren't confined to Wright-Patterson. Dayton Municipal Airport (now Dayton International) in Vandalia hosted the 1953 National Aircraft Show from September 5-7. Falling on the golden anniversary of powered flight and Ohio's sesquicentennial, the three-day event featured spectacular aircraft displays, flying demonstrations, and trophy races flown by military jet pilots. The U.S. Navy Blue Angels performed, and it was the first major show for the new USAF Thunderbirds. (The squadron estimated the crowd at 400,000, although news reports put it closer to 200,000.) Dayton outbid other cities for both the 1953 and 1954 shows; it probably didn't hurt that Air Force Secretary Harold Talbott, who attended both events, was a former Daytonian.

Fliers at those shows set records for speed, but not safety: Two Marine Corps H-19 helicopters in the 1953 show tangled rotor blades and crashed in the middle of the Airport Homes neighborhood, slightly injuring one pilot and doing minor damage to a home. In 1954, Wright Air Development Center test pilot Maj. John L. Armstrong died in a closed-course race for the General Electric cup when his F-86H Sabrejet broke up in flight. It rained debris on farmland near Tipp City and slightly injured a woman on the ground.

The national show left Dayton, but Wright-Patterson's annual open house continued, and small airports held local air fairs. The Dayton Area Chamber of Commerce began sponsoring a September "General Aviation Day" that moved between Dayton's airports in Vandalia and Miami Township.

In 1975, the chamber and Wright-Patterson officials joined forces to create a new air show that would combine the elements of civilian entertainment and military air power.

The venue was moved again to Dayton International and the weekend was changed to late July. (The base discontinued its annual open house until 2005, when the Air Force Materiel Command began the annual Freedom's Call Tattoo, held on the Friday before Independence Day. It features a festival, live music, a military award ceremony, and flybys.)

The 1975 air show was a two-day event. A hot-air balloon rally kicked it off each morning. Flybys and aerobatic acts followed. Harold Johnson and Bob Wagner were among the local performers; national celebrities included Bill Barber, Duane Cole and Jim Franklin. Military demonstrations flew each afternoon, and the Thunderbirds closed the show. It was a true extravaganza, and it set the pattern for future years.

The new show was dubbed the Dayton Air Fair, but from the beginning, organizers hoped to make it more than that. They introduced a Friday industry day in 1978, and over the years they added infrastructure and tried different trade-show formats. But the trade show has been an elusive goal for organizers; they've come and gone since the late 1970s. At this writing, a new study has raised hopes that a properly planned trade show can succeed.

Names, organizers, and content have changed over the years, but the annual weekend air show begun in 1975 continues today. It's now called the Vectren Dayton Air Show, after its title Presented by Kroger, and presenting sponsors. It's produced by the United States Air and Trade Show Inc., a not-for-profit corporation.

If you count Huffman Prairie, air shows of one kind or another have been a part of Dayton's culture for more than a century. Ty Greenlees and I had the good luck to cover 21 years of shows together as the aviation photographer and writer for the *Dayton Daily News*. (Ty continues to cover the show; I retired from the newspaper at the end of 2006 and joined the air show's board of trustees.) We hope this book will give you a sense of the excitement, wonder and pride that we've felt at the air show throughout the years, and of why we say Dayton means air show—and air show means Dayton.

BLERIOT

The Wright brothers invented the first controllable airplane, but Europeans were quick to advance the technology. Dayton celebrated a century of powered flight for the world at its 2003 air show, in part by including this 85-year-old Bleriot XI, meticulously restored by Mikael Carlson of Malmo, Sweden. Dressed as a pioneer aviator, Carlson waved to the crowd as he flew his airplane every day of the four-day show.

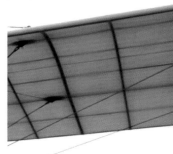

**Harriet Quimby?**
Close. Dayton native Connie Tobias, airline pilot and historical re-enactor, joined Carlson at the 2003 air show. She had flown a Bleriot and later flew a replica 1903 Wright Flyer.

A

TRIBUTE

TO

FLIGHT

**Left:** The Wright "B" Flyer has been the flying ambassador of Dayton's aviation heritage since 1982. Wright "B" Flyer Inc. owns and operates the modern look-alike of the 1911 Army Signal Corps airplane. The airplane has flown in Dayton air shows since the 1980s. What's more, it has represented Dayton across the country and overseas: It was displayed at Tempelhof Airport in Berlin in 1990 and circled the Statue of Liberty in 2003. In 2008, Wright "B" volunteers began building a new look-alike that could be packed into a standard cargo container and shipped to air shows around the world.

**Right:** John Warlick, co-founder and first pilot of the Wright "B" Flyer, wears an Army Signal Corps uniform at Dayton air shows; he was all smiles in this 1999 photo.

# JUMPERS

Squinting into the sun, you search for the silhouetted shape of an airplane some 12,000 feet above Dayton International Airport. There, you have it — just in time to see a flyspeck figure leap clear. Others follow. Moments later, they look like human meteors streaking across the sky as red smoke billows from boot-mounted flares. Down they hurtle until their high-performance, ram-air canopies blossom colorfully against the sky. This is the Flag Jump, the parachuting act that traditionally opens air shows. It's why no air show is complete without a parachute team, such as the U.S. Army's Golden Knights (right). The Dayton Air Show is no different, except in one important respect: The ripcord-type parachute is a Dayton invention, first tested over old McCook Field in 1919 and first used to save a life in 1920.

JUM

PERS

PROUD

TO

BE

AN

AMERICAN

**Left:** Marking a half-century since the invasion of Normandy, more than 450 paratroopers from the Army's 82nd Airborne Division staged a mock assault on the 1994 air show. The massive jump was made from nine low-flying Air Force transports—six C-141s and three C-130s.

**Center:** The G.I. Joe Heroes Skydiving Team celebrated the Hasbro action doll's 30th anniversary in 1994. This close-up view shows the cells of the high-performance, ram-air parachute used by air show teams. When the parachute is deployed, openings on the leading edge of the parachute scoop up air, inflating the canopy to form an airfoil shape.

**Right:** Doug Gipe of Omaha, Nebraska, manager of the Liberty Parachute Team, made the flag jump for the 2003 air show.

The U.S. Army Parachute Team, the Golden Knights, is the premiere air show parachuting act. The team was first formed in 1959, and the Army gave it official status in 1961. A Golden Knights team has jumped at most Dayton air shows since the current show was organized in 1975. Since 1985, the Golden Knights has used a C-31 (Fokker F-27) Friendship as its transport and jump plane, shown here at the 2000 air show.

**The Golden Knights** are active-duty Army parachutists, but their air show jumping is hardly standard: These pictures from the 2000 air show illustrate how they link together in mid-air to perform complex maneuvers—even upside-down.

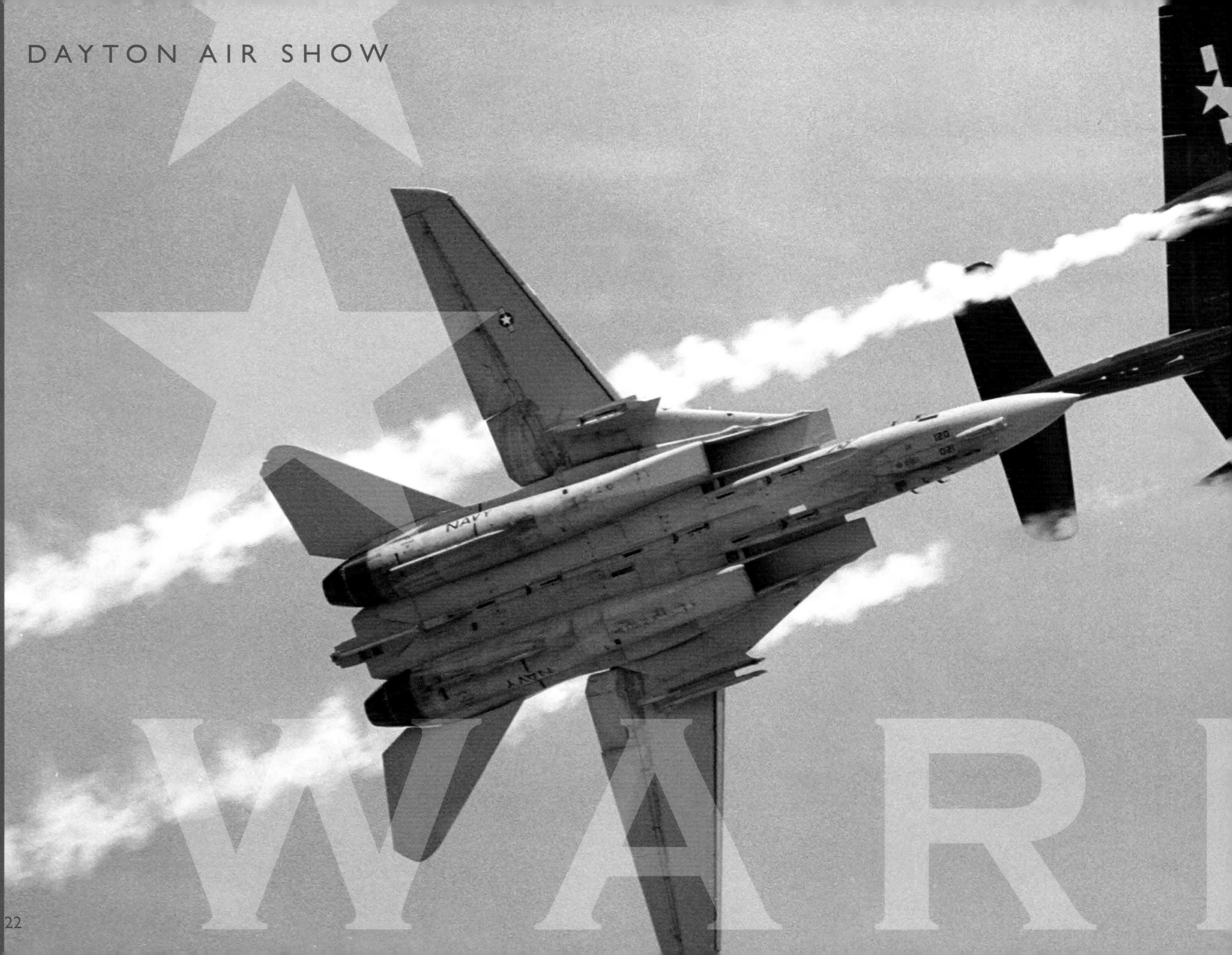
NAVY
NAVY
WAR

# W A R B I R D S

Every air show has a strong military presence. Military jet demonstrations showcase aeronautical technology and military readiness. Historic military aircraft, dubbed warbirds, reflect the valor and sacrifice of airmen in past wars. Legacy or heritage flights combine the two by flying modern and World War II aircraft in formation. In 1985, the Kalamazoo Air Museum in Michigan began the "Flight of the Cats"— formations of historic Grumman warbirds with feline names. Dale Snodgrass, a Navy pilot flying the Grumman F-14 Tomcat, added a modern "cat" to the mix. In 1996, he teamed up with John Ellis, who flew the Air Museum's F7F Tigercat in Dayton and other air shows. Snodgrass says their "Flight of the Twin-Engine Cats," shown here, was the first aerobatic legacy flight, with barrel rolls and Cuban-eights. Since the 1990s, formation flights that include both modern and historic warbirds have become air show staples.

The 2001 air show saw three jet warbirds together: a rare, Soviet-era MiG-15 (below, center middle, and right), a North American F-86 Sabre Jet (center background), and a de Havilland Sea Venom (center, wing in foreground).

This wasn't the first MiG-15 to come here. In 1953, intelligence personnel at Wright-Patterson Air Force Base received a North Korean defector's MiG-15 for analysis. Foreign technology analysis continues to be a Wright-Patterson mission with the National Air and Space Intelligence Center.

**Left and right top:** Heavy bombers of World War II vintage take constant work to keep them mechanically and aesthetically sound. This Consolidated B-24J Liberator bomber, dubbed "Joe," got its nose art touched up in preparation for a static display at the 1992 air show.

**Right bottom and far right top:** The Commemorative Air Force flew this Consolidated LB-30 as the B-24 "Diamond Lil" for many years. It was a familiar sight at Dayton air shows. The oldest B-24-type airplane flying, it was the 25th Liberator of more than 18,000 built. In real life, it was wrecked before it saw military service; Consolidated rebuilt it as a transport and renumbered it as AM-927. In 2007, CAF restored the plane to its original configuration and nickname—Old 927.

**Far right bottom:** The Mid-Atlantic Air Museum's Mitchell B-25J Briefing Time brought the distinctive sight and sound of the twin-engine medium bomber. More than 11,000 B-25s were built and figured in many battles of World War II. But the airplane gained fame as the first to bomb Japan's home islands after Japan's sneak attack on American forces in Hawaii. Lt. Col. (later Gen.) James "Jimmy" Doolittle, a former McCook Field test pilot, led the 16-plane raid from the aircraft carrier U.S.S. Hornet on April 18, 1942.

DIAMOND 'LIL'

SERVICE THIS AIRPLANE WITH
100 OCTANE FUEL ONLY
IN CASE OF EMERGENCY THE NEXT
HIGHEST GRADE WILL BE USED

1940: BUILT BY CONSOLIDATED
AIRCRAFT CORPORATION OF SAN DIEGO

1997: REFURBISHED BY LOCKHEED MARTIN
AND VOLUNTEERS OF FORT WORTH AVIATION
HERITAGE ASSOCIATION

DO NOT TURN NOSE
WHEEL MORE THAN
30 DEGREES WHEN
TOWING.

2001 HEAVY MAINTENANCE CHECK
2002 AND REFURBISHMENT BY
2003 VOLUNTEERS OF TULSA, OK.
and AMERICAN AIRLINES

Helen

AIRPLANE COMMANDER
Bus TAYLOR
CREW CHIEF
Joe MOORE

BRIEFING TIME

BOMBARDIER
Ken CLAUSSEN
NAVIGATOR
Bob FRENCH

ENGINE
PR

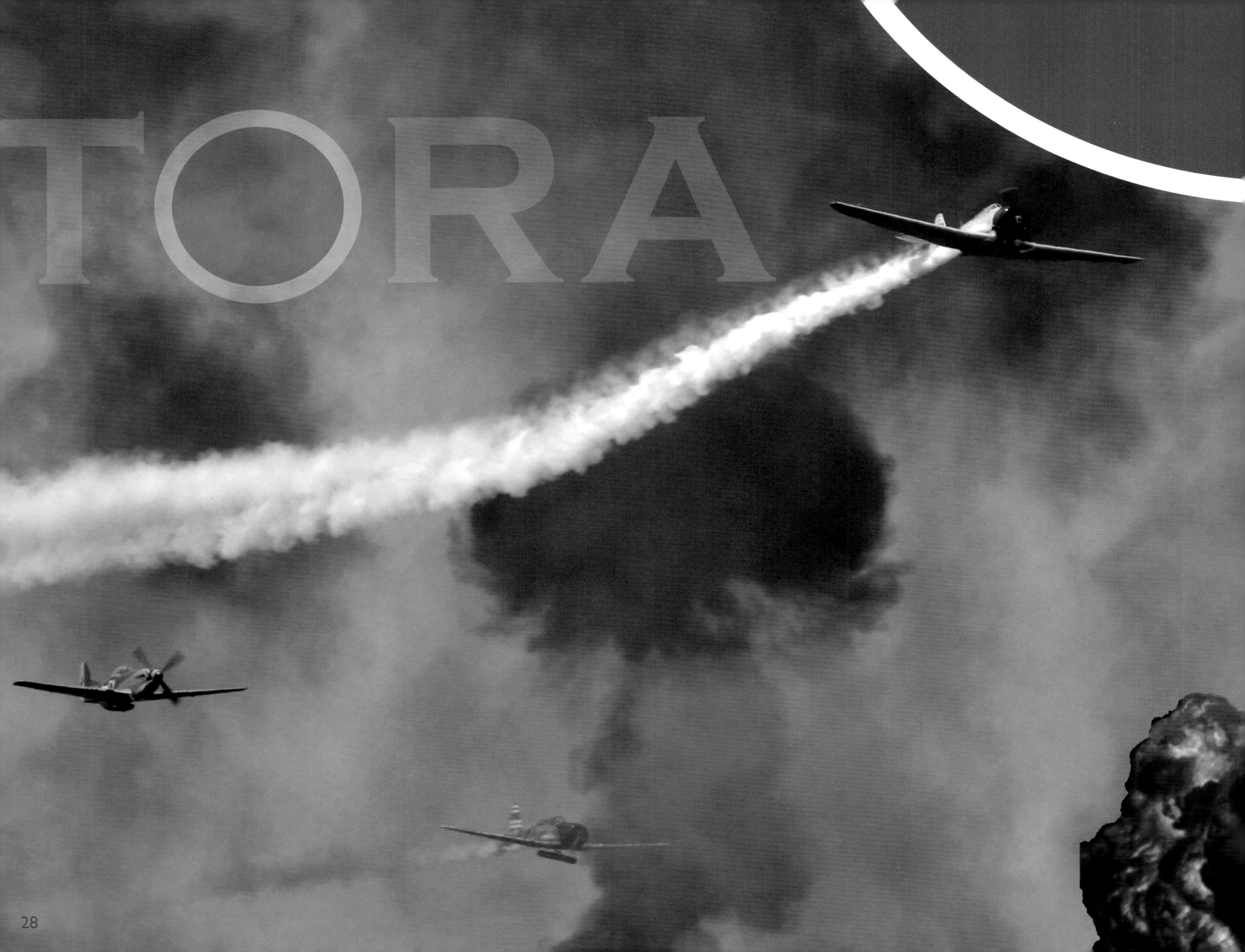
TORA

A sudden boom sweeps across the air show crowd. Heads turn as a siren wails and black smoke rises. The announcer transports everyone back to December 7, 1941, the day of Japan's infamous attack on U.S. Forces in Hawaii. "Tora! Tora! Tora!" was a 1970 20th Century Fox film about the attack. The film used modified American AT-6 and BT-13 airplanes to resemble Japanese warbirds. After the filming, six of the aircraft were donated to the Confederate Air Force (later Commemorative Air Force.) CAF volunteers began using the planes to re-enact the attack for air show audiences. Today, the act involves many volunteers, careful planning and elaborate preparation to execute a safe but thrilling event. It's arguably the most popular civilian air show act ever staged. As the "Tora" team demonstrated here in the 2002 air show, the act has all the elements a crowd craves: fiery explosions, rattling machine guns, growling engines, and dogfighting airplanes. But it's more than that.

**Filmed** before the era of computer graphics, "Tora's" epic battle scenes required real airplanes. Japanese "Kates" (right and below, in the 1988 air show) were crafted from the front ends of North American AT-6 Texans and the tails of Vultee BT-13s. Japanese "Zeroes" (far right, in 1991) were modified Texans.

**To the pilots** who fly in it, "Tora" is more than entertainment; it's a living history lesson for generations who only know about the horrific raid on Pearl Harbor through books or their grandparents' stories.

# TORA

The same is true of all who restore, maintain and fly warbirds. They are not just flying fancy planes. They are telling a story.

**The heavy bombers** of World War II are among the rarest warbirds still flying – not only few in numbers, but challenging to maintain and expensive to fuel with four piston engines guzzling aviation-grade gasoline. The groups that fly them depend on skilled volunteers to keep them airworthy.

Just a handful of **B-24s, B-17s** and Avro Lancasters still make it to air shows.

The 1992
air show featured the B-17G Fuddy Duddy.
The view from the bombardier's seat in the airplane's nose (over
Dayton on a tour in 2004) was almost dizzying.

**Left:** The Avro Lancaster was the British Royal Air Force's main heavy bomber
of World War II. It was built mainly in Britain, but several hundred were produced in
Canada. At last report, only two Lancasters remained airworthy—one in England and one
in Canada. In 1994, the Canadian Warplane Heritage Museum brought North America's
only flying Lancaster to the air show.

Silhouetted against a blazing sun, the Commemorative Air Force's Boeing B-29 "Fifi" (left) and the B-24 Diamond Lil (right) made a rare sight in the sky over the 1994 air show. That year saw four World War II heavy bombers at the show—a B-29, B-24, B-17, and Avro Lancaster. The air shows in the first half of the 1990s emphasized warbirds to mark the 50th anniversary of World War II.

**Restored airplanes** can paint a nostalgic and all-too-romantic picture of World War II. Inside their metal skins were young men who hoped to survive the war and live in peace. Many didn't. In 1994, a local group called the Association of Living History put a human face on the warbird displays by posing as World War II fliers or flight nurses. Each volunteer carefully researched the position he or she represented, then put together an authentic uniform for that position. Suffering in lined leather jackets in the summer heat, they answered questions about their duties and gear. "We act as a living memorial to the veterans," Association President Troy Mulvaine said.

"Fifi" was the world's only flying B-29 in 1994 when it paid its first—and so far only—visit to the air show. Worn-out engines grounded it in 2006. More than $1 million has been raised to re-engine it. Another B-29 restoration is underway in Wichita, Kansas.

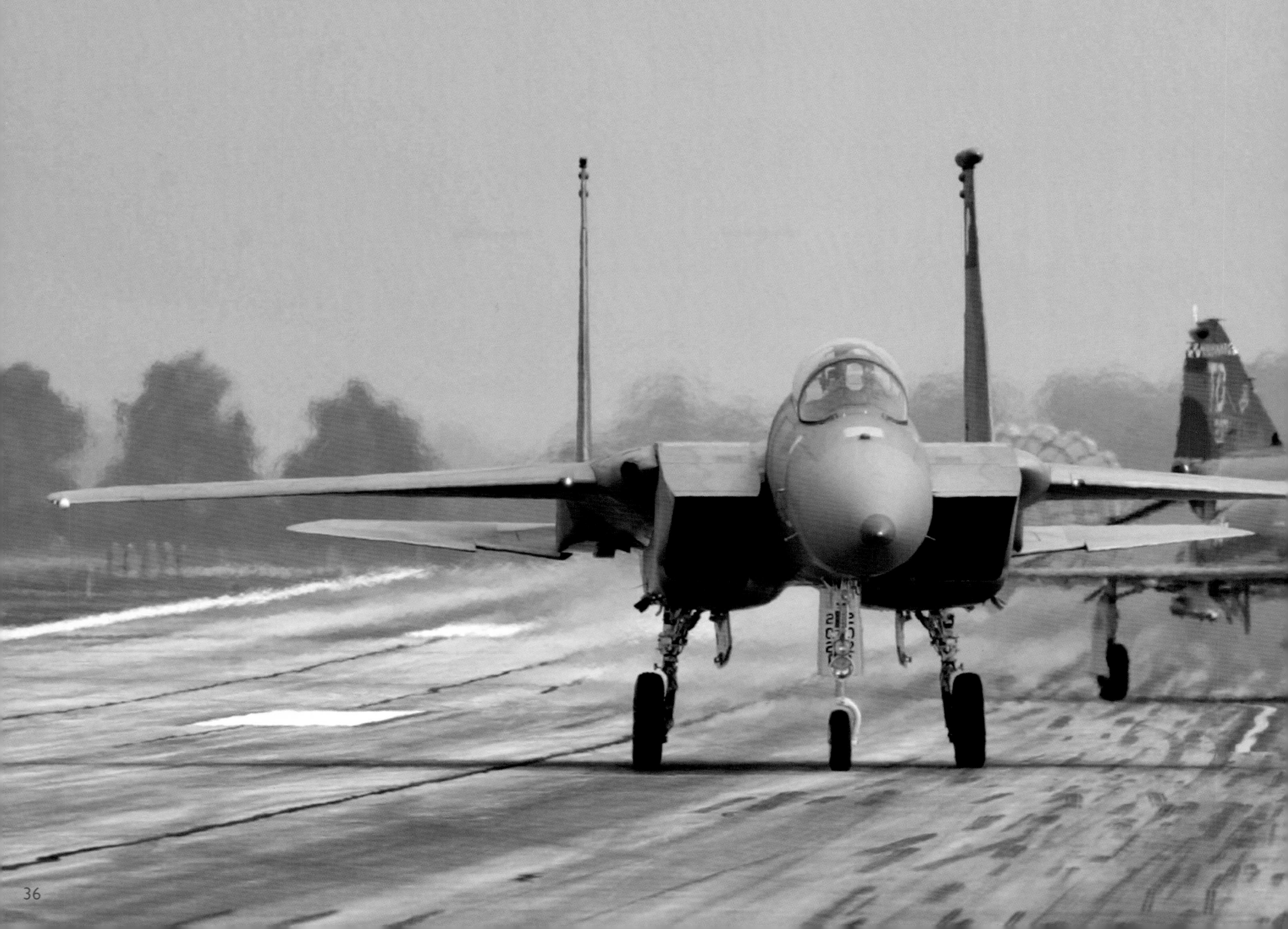

Two generations of fighter jets shared the runway in the 2007 air show following a heritage flight with a World War II-era, North American P-51 Mustang. The Boeing F-15C Eagle (foreground) replaced the Vietnam war-era McDonnell Douglas F-4 Phantom II (background, trailing a dragchute) as the Air Force's frontline fighter jet; the stealthy Lockheed Martin F-22A Raptor is replacing the Eagle. The Air Force no longer flies the Phantom; this QF-4E is flown under contract as a training target.

**Legacy and heritage flights** are popular in Dayton as elsewhere.

**Clockwise from left:** Three Mustangs of the Horsemen, accompanied by an F-15 (not in picture) in 2003; A Fairchild Republic A-10 Thunderbolt II leads a Republic P-47 Thunderbolt and P-51 Mustang in 1999; an F-15 Eagle escorts the Lockheed P-38 Lightning Porky II in 2005; a P-51 is flanked by a QF-4E and F-15 (left wingtip in picture) in 2007, and a Vought F-4U Corsair and Boeing F/A-18 Hornet, also in 2007.

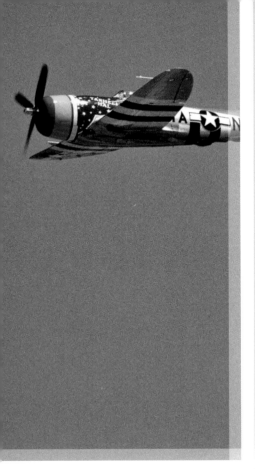

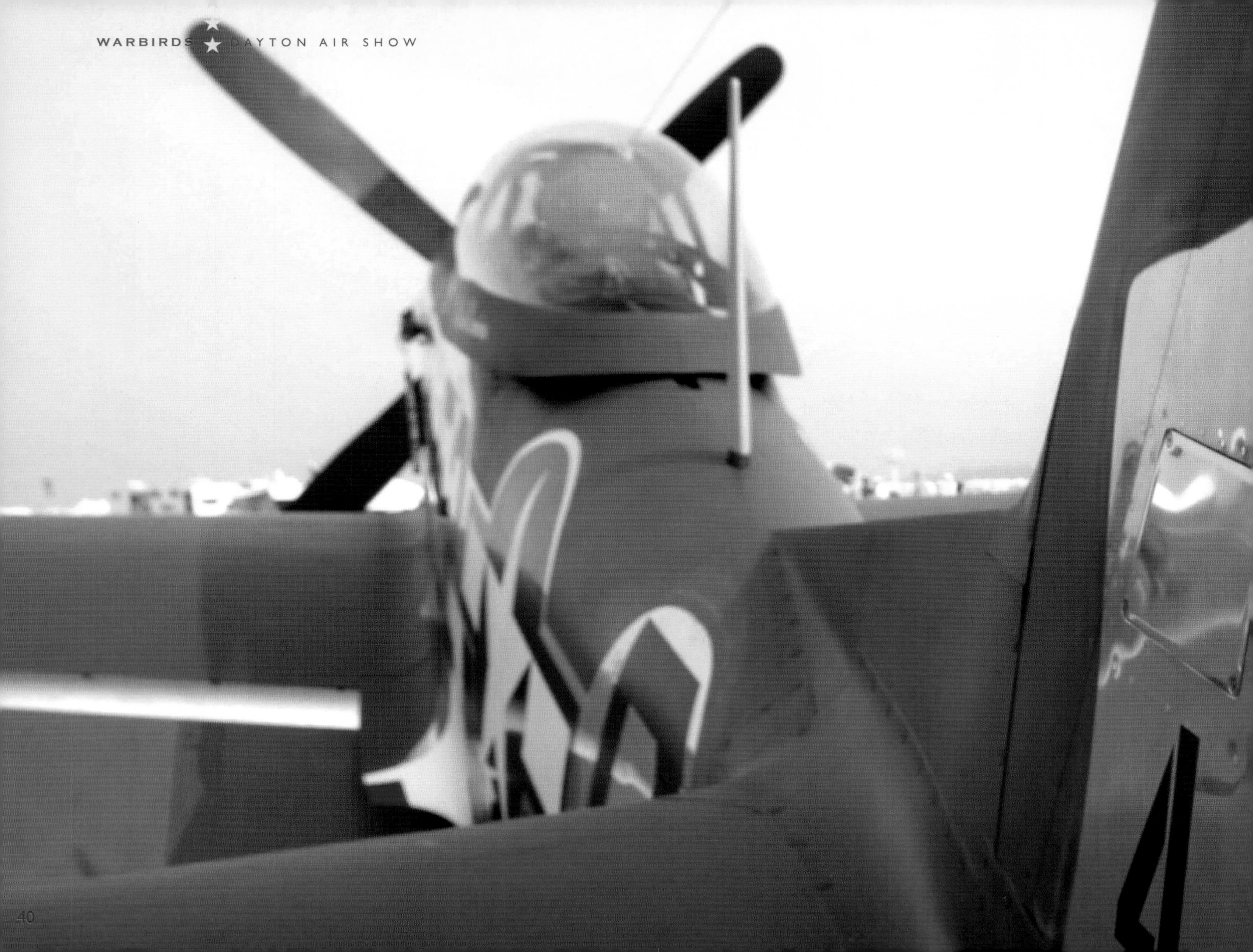

From 2002 through 2005, Rolls Royce of North America and the National Aviation Hall of Fame brought a prestigious competition to the air show. The Eastern Region Invitational gave warbird owners in the eastern half of the United States a chance to win a Rolls Royce Heritage Trophy like one awarded each year in the National Aviation Heritage Invitational at the Reno Air Races in Nevada. The Eastern Region contest brought museum-quality warbirds to the Dayton Air Show. The People's Choice Award in 2002 went to Chuck Greenhill's P-51D Geraldine, shown here.

# MILITARY JETS

Military jets are an important element in all major air shows, but they have special significance to Dayton's. Almost every Air Force jet flying had its start in a procurement or technology program at Wright-Patterson Air Force Base, including the Northrop Grumman B-2 Spirit bomber shown here at the 1994 air show. Military jet demonstrations have been a Dayton Air Show staple since its first Air Fair in 1975. Military craft in that year's event included an AV-8A Harrier, F-100 Super Sabre, F-15 Eagle, A-7 Corsair IIs, and a C-123 transport plane that dropped cargo as well as paratroopers.

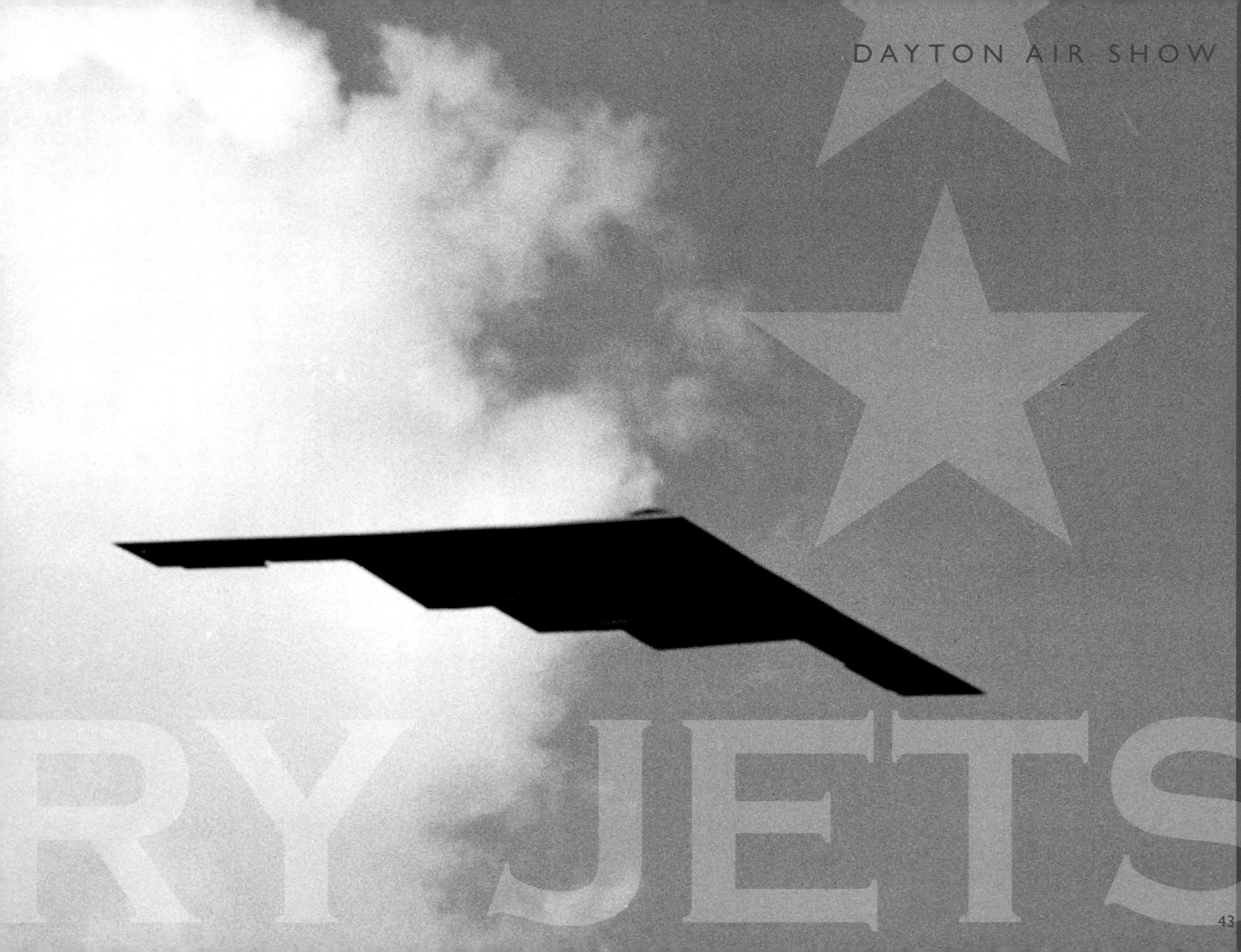
RY JETS

SR71

**Exotic** is the only word that describes the
Lockheed SR-71 Blackbird. Designed for supersonic spy missions, the SR-71 could fly at least
2,200 miles per hour—Mach 3.2—and exceed
80,000 feet above sea level. Even on static
display, a Blackbird drew crowds—as this one
did at Dayton's 1985 show.

The SR-71 has several nicknames, but one—the Sled—was made popular by the pilot who flew this one to the 1985 show: Maj. Brian Shul, who would later author the 1992 book *Sled Driver*. Shul's stint flying the world's most exotic military jet capped a remarkable career that included narrowly surviving a fiery crash when his AT-28 was shot down on his 212th combat mission in Southeast Asia. *Sled Driver*, Shul's first book, quickly became an aviation classic. His reconnaissance systems officer on this visit (seen in the back seat) was Col. Walter Watson Jr., the only African-American to hold an SR-71 aircrew position. Shul and Watson later co-authored *The Untouchables*, another book about flying the SR-71.

Although the SR-71 first flew in 1964 and was derived from the earlier A-12, the airplane still looked like something out of science fiction in 1985. Sadly for aviation buffs, you won't see this again: The last flying SR-71 landed forever in October 1999.

Whenever a **Boeing B-52** Stratofortress visits the Dayton Air Show, it's a kind of homecoming: In October 1948, six Boeing engineers designed the airplane over a long weekend in Dayton's Van Cleve Hotel. Boeing had offered the Air Force a straight-wing, turboprop bomber, but Col. Henry "Pete" Warden, chief of bomber development at Wright Field, pressed them for something befitting the jet age. The result was one of history's most enduring aircraft designs.

It's short, plump, and its wings and tail droop. But the McDonnell Douglas (now Boeing/BAE) AV-8B Harrier II can rise straight up from the ground, hover, turn, and even back up. And the Marine Corps' "Jump-jet" is incredibly noisy. No wonder every air show wants a Harrier demo.

**The Harrier** is an old air show favorite. The first Dayton Air Fair in 1975 featured a Hawker Siddeley AV-8A Harrier, the predecessor of the AV-8B shown here. But the Harrier's days are numbered: It's to be replaced by the stealthy, supersonic, F-35B Lightning II. The first one rolled out of Lockheed Martin's Fort Worth plant in December 2007. First delivery to the Marine Corps is slated for 2011.

49

**The wings** of a Boeing F/A-18 fighter jet stream condensation and its tailpipes glow from the heat of its afterburners at a Dayton Air Show as its pilot demonstrates the Hornet's ability to turn on a dime. Many military aviators vie for a chance to fly their aircraft to a hometown air show for static display, but only specially assigned demonstration pilots actually fly in air shows. Below: The twin-engine Boeing F-15 Eagle is another popular jet.

**The Fairchild Republic A-10** attack jet is nicknamed the Thunderbolt II, but it's better known as the Wart Hog. The ungainly-looking Air Force jet has been flying its close air support mission for more than thirty years, but it's continually updated. Above: The depleted-uranium shells of the Wart Hog's seven-barrel Gatling gun have been criticized for contaminating battlefields, but they proved effective at destroying Iraqi tanks.

Stealth technology emerged from the shadows of secrecy at the 1990 air show with the first visit by a Lockheed Martin F-117A Nighthawk. Below: Former Clayton resident Col. John Zink brought an F-117A to Dayton in 1990, the first year the jets appeared at air shows. He flew an airplane assigned to 37th Fighter Wing Commander Col. (later Brig. Gen.) Tony Tolin.

COL TONY TOLIN

The Northrop Grumman B-2 Spirit has made several flybys at Dayton air shows. Each pass by the relatively quiet, four-engine bomber is an eerie experience: Sculpted to deflect radar beams, it seems to change shape as it goes by.

**Top left:** The Ohio Air National Guard Base in Springfield has always supported Dayton air shows. Here, a flight of Lockheed Martin F-16Cs from the 178th Fighter Wing at Springfield makes a pass. The unit specializes in training U.S. and foreign F-16 pilots.

**Top right:** Navy Lt. Cdr. Paul "Bobo" Felini, a West Chester native, flew this Boeing F/A-18C Hornet at the 2007 show; his sister, Lt. Page "Pie" Felini, brought a Super Hornet for static display. Both were from VFA-106, the "Gladiators."

**Bottom left:** Thousands were built, but the McDonnell Douglas F-4 Phantom II is a rare sight now. The Air Force used this QF-4E as a training target. Maj. Chris Vance flew it at the 2007 show.

**Bottom right:** A swing-wing Boeing B-1B Lancer bomber tucked its wings and lit its afterburners for a fast, thunderous flyby at the 1996 air show.

**Below:** The Lockheed Martin F-16 is officially nicknamed Fighting Falcon, but its pilots have always favored "Viper." This F-16C pilot from the Viper East demonstration team flew at the 2006 air show.

# STARFIGHTERS

Rick Svetkoff's **Starfighters F-104** Demo Team of Clearwater, Florida, flies three restored Canadian versions of the dart-like Lockheed jet. Small and fast—the first operational fighter that could fly at twice the speed of sound—the F-104 still gives an impressive ride. Author Tim Gaffney learned this firsthand at the 1998 air show when Crew Chief Drew Holmes (standing) strapped him into a CF-104D behind Tom Delashaw, Svetkoff's partner. Seated far ahead of the stubby wings, the sensation was like riding on the tip of an arrow—one with a howling afterburner.

CAPT. RICK SVETKOFF

RESCUE
OTHER SIDE

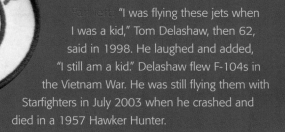

"I was flying these jets when I was a kid," Tom Delashaw, then 62, said in 1998. He laughed and added, "I still am a kid." Delashaw flew F-104s in the Vietnam War. He was still flying them with Starfighters in July 2003 when he crashed and died in a 1957 Hawker Hunter.

Steel spurs connect to cables that will jerk the pilot's legs back against the seat in an ejection. Crew Chief Drew Holmes (right) keeps the Starfighters in flying shape.

STARFIGHTERS

# ON THE GROUND

Right up against the fence is where the most passionate fans plant themselves at a weekend air show, as these young spectators did in 1996. But aerial acts are only one element of the air show's fare. Aircraft static displays allow visitors a closeup look at America's most advanced military aircraft and a chance to talk to their crews. Other static aircraft typically include World War II-era warbirds, helicopters, antique airplanes, and even homebuilt aircraft. Over the years, non-flying acts have included jet-propelled trucks, flame-snorting mechanical monsters and, one year, a World War II-vintage Sherman tank. Trade shows from the late 1970s to mid-1990s offered as many as four days of aerospace industry events. The 2003 and 2004 air shows included a 20,000-square-foot museum in a tent—the Birthplace of Aviation Pavilion, which featured a walk-through timeline of aviation history with full-size replicas of Wright flyers.

**A C-5 galaxy** dwarfed this visitor to the 1995 air show.

**Below left:** When they weren't parachuting from a C-130 Hercules, soldiers with the Army's 82nd Airborne Division seldom just walked at the 1991 air show.

After a flight from South America, the crew of this Brazilian Air Force C-130 prepped the airplane for static display in the 2007 air show. Right: A KC-10 (foreground), B-52, C-5 and C-141 made up a display of heavies in 1992.

Powered by three Pratt & Whitney J34-48 jet engines, Les Shockley's Shockwave jet truck tops 300 miles per hour in flame-belching dashes down the runway. Les and his son Kent built the truck for drag racing in the 1980s, but it's always in demand by air shows. Familiar to Dayton air show crowds, Shockwave returned in 2004 with the Masters of Disaster, a wild barnstorming act that included the truck and three dueling biplanes flown by Jim Franklin, Jim LeRoy and Bobby Younkin.

Firing blank cannon rounds, A World War II-vintage Sherman tank did battle with Robosaurus, a 40-foot-tall mechanical monster, at the 1995 air show. The duel wasn't planned: when the tank arrived too late for an aerial battle re-enactment, its crew decided to ad-lib a fight with Robosaurus.

# ROAR

Surrounded by color, this aeronaut prepared his hot-air balloon for an evening flight in 1987. For many years, the air show started as early as 7 a.m. with a mass balloon launch. Balloonists sometimes gave Friday evening preview flights for the news media. Ballooning has moved south: Middletown hosted the U.S. National Hot Air Balloon Championships in 1992, '93 and '94, and balloon contests returned to Middletown with the first annual MidFirst Ohio Challenge in 2003.

Air Force heavy aircraft dominate the static display of every air show. Left: a C-5 Galaxy caught the morning sun in 1984.

Still deadly after all these years, a B-52 bomber arrived at the 2006 air show. Designed for nuclear warfare with the Soviet Union in the 1950s, the Stratofortress has been upgraded into a precision-bombing platform. Equipped with eight engines and warty with sensor fairings, the B-52 is nicknamed "BUFF," for Big Ugly Fat... ah, Fellow.

Always a strong supporter of the Dayton Air Show, the 445th Airlift Wing turned this C-5 Galaxy into a walk-through exhibit for the 2006 air show. The Air Force Reserve unit is based at Wright-Patterson Air Force Base and flew C-141 Starlifters before converting to the C-5.

**Far left:** Robert Edwards, 12, of Kingston, Tennessee, found a shady place to watch the 1987 air show: under the wing of a Royal Air Force VC-10.

**Left:** Tyler Poff, 4, of London, Ohio, was wide-eyed under this flight helmet from an AH-64 Apache attack helicopter. Poff and others got to sit in the Apache while it was on display in the 2000 air show.

**Right:** Isaac Monnin, 4, of Sylvania, Ohio, jumped up for a peek into the cannon port of this F-4E Phantom II at the 2006 air show.

71

**Military,** federal, state, and local dignitaries cut the ribbon on the new exposition center in 1992. The United States Air and Trade Show that year included a four-day industry expo in addition to the weekend air show. The trade show fizzled after a few years, but the idea continues to draw interest.

**Left:** A grownup's shoulders can make a great perch for a youngster at an air show.

**Center:** History was on display at the 2003 air show. Lon Frampton of DeKalb, Illinois, inspected Mikael Carlson's Tumelisa, a World War I-era fighter-trainer from Sweden. The antique airplanes were a part of airport director and air show trustee Blair Conrad's efforts to make Dayton's centennial air show a true extravaganza. He succeeded, despite an ongoing battle with cancer that finally claimed him in 2005.

**Right:** Eight wicked-looking blades sprout from the hub of this Navy E-2C Hawkeye. The carrier-based airborne warning, command and control center was a part of the 2006 air show's static display.

75

Most of the Air Force aircraft flying today are the products of research and development programs at Wright-Patterson Air Force Base. It should be no surprise that military aircraft are a major element of Dayton air shows. The A-10 Thunderbolt II, left, and the CV-22, below, both on display at the 2007 air show, are examples of the products of acquisition programs managed by the Aeronautical Systems Center at Wright-Patterson.

The 906th Fighter Group at Wright-Patterson was a common sight at Dayton air shows in the 1980s and early '90s before it was replaced by the 445th Airlift Wing. Besides putting their F-4 Phantom and later F-16 fighter jets on display, the unit would give weapons-loading demonstrations. Here a crew carried a missile to a waiting jet. The blue band on its body indicated that the weapon was a training dummy.

Dave VanLiere brought his deHavilland Sea Venom to the 2001 air show. The folding wings signaled it was the naval version of the Royal Air Force's DH 112 Venom.

# SOLO PILOT

Solo pilots are the rock stars of the air show business. They get the aerial stage to themselves, sometimes performing before tens of thousands of spectators. Dayton has always enjoyed the top solo air show pilots—Duane Cole and Jimmy Franklin, legends of the air show circuit, flew in the first Dayton Air Fair in 1975. The best pilots become more than entertainers—they help shape the air show industry, influence sport aviation overall and work outside the cockpit to train, mentor, and inspire others in the world of flight. Such a pilot is Sean D. Tucker, shown here flying his custom-made Challenger II biplane in the 2003 air show. Tucker's accomplishments made him a 2008 enshrinee in the National Aviation Hall of Fame. He is only the second active air show pilot so honored: Patty Wagstaff, another pilot familiar to Dayton, was enshrined in 2004.

SOLO

PILOT

A popular solo performer at Dayton air shows since 1993, Tucker flew for a record crowd in Dayton's four-day Centennial of Flight air show in 2003. The top wing displays the name of his sponsor, Oracle Corp.

Seldom standing still, Tucker paused for this 2003 portrait with the Challenger II. He has named each of his air show planes Challenger. Why? "I call it the Challenger because every time I get in the airplane, it reminds me to challenge myself in the sky."

Constant training makes an aerobatic airplane almost an extension of the pilot's body. "I feel like it's a part of me," Tucker says. "I feel like the wings are my arms. I feel like when I touch that airplane, I'm using my arms to make the designs in the sky... I consider it a dance."

**The stars** were aligned for this photo—air show stars Tucker and Wagstaff, paired up for a photo flight in advance of the 2003 air show.

STEVE &

**Formation-flying** with his hands, Tucker works out the plan for a photo flight with Wagstaff before leaving the ground at the 2003 air show. Aviation photographers prize air-to-air pictures, and Tucker's announcer, Brian Norris, is widely regarded as the best camera-plane pilot in the air show business.

SMITHSONIAN
EST. 1846

**Patty Wagstaff** made her name in competition even as her air show star was rising: She became the first woman to win the U.S. Aerobatic Championship in 1991, a feat she repeated in 1992 and '93. Her airplane in those contests, an Extra 260, now hangs in the National Air and Space Museum. Wagstaff flew in her first Dayton air show in 1989, and she has returned often. Her 2004 appearance included another Dayton event—enshrinement in the National Aviation Hall of Fame, which lauded her for breaking gender barriers in aviation. Wagstaff says her greatest joy comes from letters and emails from young people who say she inspired them to fly. "Those kind of things make it feel like you are on a bigger mission, and [make you] realize that the importance of air shows is more than just about entertainment."

"I love flying formation," Wagstaff says, but she asserts that a solo pilot has more freedom. "In a solo act, the pilot is capable of doing much more aerobatics than possible in a formation act."

NATIONAL
HALL
Patty Wagstaff
GOODRICH
USA
AEROBATIC TEAM
N3300G
Flight Simulator

**Left:** "Women in Aviation" was the 2004 air show's theme, and four female pilots formed up for this photo flight: Wagstaff in her Extra 300S; Debbie Gary in her Marchetti F26OD; Julie Clark in her Beech T-34 Mentor, and Reno air racer Mary Dilda in her North American SNJ Two of Hearts. It was also the weekend Wagstaff was inducted into the National Aviation Hall of Fame, and she lost no time putting the hall of fame logo on her airplane, just behind the canopy.

**Right:** Even a solo pilot needs ground support. Melissa Courtney, an instructor and aerobatic pilot, was Wagstaff's assistant for several years. Enthusiastic spectators put grins on their faces at the 2002 air show.

*Wagstaff* has lived all over the world. In 1996, Ty Greenlees photographed her at Avra Valley Airport near Tucson, Arizona, where she lived then. She later moved to Florida.

WAGSTA

"Gypsy" is Wagstaff's nickname among air show friends. "I'm so independent and love to come and go as I want," she says. She set up her own Airstream trailer park at the 1996 air show.

Left: The late Ian Groom flew in several Dayton air shows. Here he goes vertical above the airport in his Russian-built Sukhoi 31 at the 2000 show. Center: Not only a performer, Tucker mentors others—even upside down, as he was in 2004 over Miami County on a training flight with the Stars of Tomorrow, a group of up-and-coming young pilots: Tucker's son Eric, right (in biplane); Jessy Panzer, left; and the late Nick Nilmeyer, in the slot position. (Nilmeyer died in a landing accident in 2006.)

**Teresa Stokes** is a noted aviation artist and the glamorous wingwalker on Gene Soucy's big Grumman Showcat biplane. She once saved Soucy's life by donating a kidney when his were failing, and tests of his own family members failed to find a compatible donor. But she pulls line duty when Soucy flies a solo act. Here she pumped smoke oil into Soucy's Extra 300S at the 1998 air show.

**Left:** Harold Johnson, the "Flying Mayor of Moraine," flew in many Dayton air shows from the 1960s into the '90s. He flew this red WACO biplane in the 1991 show. An old-fashioned barnstormer at heart, Johnson was one of several hometown pilots who added a local flavor to Dayton air shows in the 1970s and '80s.

**Below:** Debbie Gary flew her first Dayton air show in 1977 in a Bellanca Super Viking. She was back in 2004, in this bright yellow Marchetti F26OD.

**Top right and bottom right:** Skip Stewart in his biplane Prometheus (top) brought a high-energy style to the 2007 air show. He flew an act called "Code Name: Mary's Lamb" with Jim LeRoy (bottom). It was a new form of air show act—one that combined old-fashioned barnstorming with a science fiction storyline. Tragically, LeRoy crashed in his biplane Bulldog II during Saturday's show—the air show's only fatal crash since it began in 1975. On Sunday, Stewart flew a tribute to his fallen friend.

**Far right:** A legend among legends, the late Leo Loudenslager was a seven-time national aerobatic champion and the 1980 World Aerobatic Champion. His Loudenslager Stevens Akro Laser 200 monoplane hangs in the National Air and Space Museum. He was also known for the bullet-shaped Bud Light Microjet he flew, as he did here in the 1992 air show.

Air shows are about entertainment and showmanship, while aerobatic contests are about skill and competition. Beginning in 1998, air show promoters staged a new kind of contest, using air shows as the venue for competition by the world's best air show pilots. The Championship Air Show Pilots Association created the CASPA Challenge, with top pilots competing in a series of events at air shows in Dayton; Cleveland; Oshkosh, Wisconsin, and once in Detroit. The series continued through 2001. Four contenders formed up in 2000 for this photo: Sean D. Tucker (in an earlier airplane and color scheme), Rocky Hill, Michael Goulian, and Gene Soucy.

A blue sky is the perfect air show backdrop, but clouds can give the sky definition when the air is otherwise clear. The clouds seemed to beckon Tucker and Ian Groom in this 1996 photo.

DAREDEVILS

...gstaff and helpers push her Extra 300 out of the McCauley Propeller Systems hangar at the 1996 air show. The McCauley hangar sheltered air show planes for years until parent company Cessna moved its propeller unit to Georgia in 2002.

Early air shows were sometimes called air carnivals or circuses. Civilian teams can bring that old-fashioned carnival flavor to an air show—especially wingwalkers, who perform such daredevil stunts as cavorting between the wings of a biplane, climbing from one aircraft onto another, or balancing precariously on a tiny ultralight, as Jon Falkner did here on Bob Essell's Quicksilver ultralight in 2001. Formation teams bring a smoother style to the show. Much of it has to do with the art of formation flying, which emphasizes harmony and precision. Not that formation flying can't be thrilling—an opposing pass or crossover, done with split-second timing, can leave a crowd slack-jawed. But formation maneuvers that trace graceful patterns across the sky can add a touch of elegance to an air show.

N2250Y

**Left:** The Stars of Tomorrow flew planes designed for competition aerobatics. Below: Flying World War II-era Stearman biplanes, the Red Baron Pizza Squadron thrilled millions over 28 years before being disbanded in 2007.

With gliderlike wings and small
engines, the Fouga CM-170 Magister
emphasizes grace over power. The U.S. Jet
Aerobatic Team flew three Magisters in the 2004
air show. Johnny Hutchison (far right) flew right wing
to his brother Rob. Jim Hayhurst was the lead pilot. Only a
very few civilian air show teams fly jets.

**A French design,** the Magister was built in the 1950s as a trainer. Rob Hutchison said the airplane's lines reflect its sailplane heritage. "It's a very easy airplane to fly and it lends itself to flying formation aerobatics," he said.

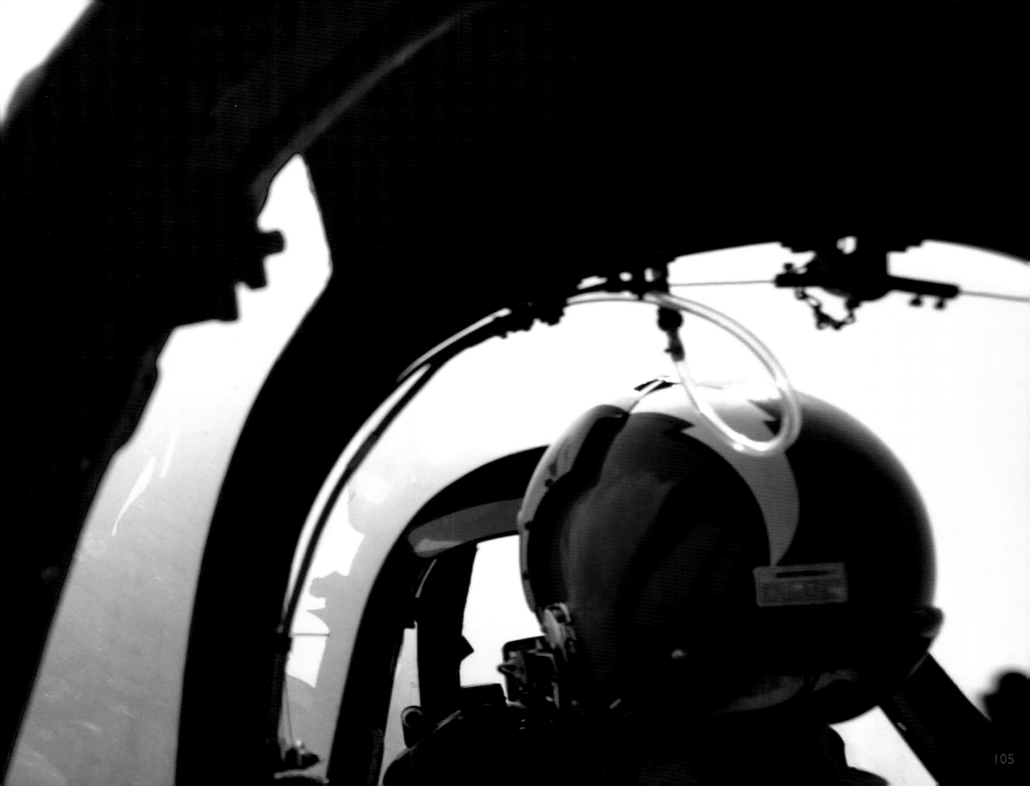

Designed for aerobatics, the Pitts biplane has been a staple of air shows since the 1970s. Many of the air show circuit's top pilots learned aerobatics in a Pitts, and some have evolved the basic Pitts design into highly customized aircraft such as Sean D. Tucker's Oracle Challenger. The Pitts is a small airplane, but bright colors and plenty of airshow smoke can make them seem bigger—and a four-ship formation can give them a major presence. The Holiday Inn Aerobatic Team started as a three-ship team called the Blackhawks in the early 1980s, added a fourth Pitts and gained Holiday Inn as a sponsor. They showed their colors in the 1990 air show. The team became the Holiday Inn/Coca-Cola Aerobatic Team in 1991 and disbanded in 1993 after the death of team leader T. J. Brown.

Daniel Heligoin and Montaine Mallet delighted crowds for more than 26 years with the **romantic aerial duet** they dubbed "the French Connection." Their act, last performed at the Dayton Air Show in 1995, was noted for its custom music and their own recorded narration. Tragically, they died during a training flight in 2000.

107

**Old-fashioned** barnstorming is at the heart of John Mohr's air show routines. At the 1995 air show he demonstrated a new act he'd just perfected two years earlier: flying his 1943 Stearman PT-17 with flawless precision while stuntman Royce Baar climbed from the Stearman's wing to an Enstrom helicopter. Mohr also flies the Stearman and helicopter in solo performances—but only one at a time.

**Pat Wagner** calls her specialty wingriding instead of wingwalking because she remains strapped to a mast atop the airplane. It's the best place to see an air show, she said in 1999. "I have the best view of anybody. ... Sometimes you can identify the kids and the people waving things." The position feels surprisingly secure, she said. "I feel like I'm part of the airplane." Well, most of the time: In an inverted pass, "You don't feel like you're on the airplane. You feel like you're hanging from it." Riding on a wing is more than a wind-in-the-hair experience. At late-summer air shows, Pat said she could feel the sting of grasshoppers smacking against her flight suit.

Bob and Pat Wagner have been on the sir show scene since the 1960s. Pat rode on their Stearman biplane as the "Girl on the Wing" in the first Dayton Air Fair in 1975. In 1999, the Experimental Aircraft Association honored Pat for 25 years as an air show wingwalker. Bob is also known for flying the Goodrich Linco Taperwing, a one-of-a-kind 1929 WACO biplane, at air show openings.

109

Teresa Stokes is a petite woman, but she looks larger than life between the wings of the brawny Showcat, a Grumman Ag Cat crop sprayer modified for air show flying. Wearing stiletto-heel boots, she climbs about the burly biplane while Gene Soucy flies it. An aerobatic pilot herself, Stokes likes things that go: She restores classic cars and even lives on a houseboat in Houston, Texas. Gene Soucy has been a professional air show pilot since 1968 and is one of the most respected figures in the business. Ty Greenlees captured them over Dayton in 1995 with a wing-mounted camera.

In the 1920s and '30s, the WACO Aircraft Co. in Troy, Ohio, turned out thousands of gorgeous biplanes—but never one with a jet engine strapped to its belly. Air show legend Jimmy Franklin added that feature to his WACO UPF-7 in 1999 and flew it with his son Kyle as wingwalker. Roaring like a space shuttle, the old biplane could soar straight up on a column of smoke. The Franklins brought their jaw-dropping act to Dayton in 2004. Jimmy and the WACO were lost in a crash in 2005, but Kyle has continued the family air show tradition with his own flying act.

OKLAHOMA RACING TURBINES
COWETA, OKLAHOMA

Jimmy Franklin

# WING WALKERS

The Boeing Stearman was a training plane for Army and Navy cadets in World War II. After the war, many of the sturdy biplanes found new life as cropdusters, often beefed up with 450-horsepower engines. The extra power made them ideal air show planes, and they have been an important element of air shows for decades. Dave Dacy flew his Stearman A75 at the 1996 air show with Hollywood stuntman Johnny Kazian on the wing.

Formed in 1995, the Montreal-based Northern Lights Demonstration Team featured five pilots from four countries. Its military-style precision made the team one of North America's best. It came to Dayton in 2000.

The **Northern Lights** team in 2000: Azat Zaydullin; Michele Thonney; Mario Hamel; Andre Lortie, and Michael Mancuso. In front is crew chief Patrice Hubert.

115

Stars of Tomorrow in 2004: Eric Tucker (left), Jessy Panzer, Nick Nilmeyer.

**Sean D. Tucker** and Mike Goulian started the Stars of Tomorrow in 2003 as a way to groom a new generation of air show pilots. The program trained eight young pilots over three years. Sean's son Eric (in the blue-and-white biplane) is now a member of the Collaborators, a team Tucker formed in 2007.

ROTAR

# ROTARY WING

Fixed-wing pilots like to say, "Helicopters don't fly; they beat the air into submission." The tiltrotor V-22 Osprey does both, as this Air Force CV-22 demonstrated at the 2007 air show. The Osprey is a cross between two worlds of flight: It combines the vertical lift and hovering capability of a helicopter with the superior speed and range of an airplane. The Air Force says this combination enables its Special Operations Forces to execute missions that previously would have required both kinds of aircraft. The CV-22 is an Air Force-modified version of the Marine Corps' MV-22. The Osprey is the latest expression of a concept for flight that was first recorded by Leonardo da Vinci.

Y WING ING

"Giant bug eats truck." That would have made a fitting headline for this photo from the 1992 air show, but in fact it was a Sikorsky CH-54 Tarhe, demonstrating its heavy-lift capability by hauling an Army vehicle through the air. The Army used the Tarhe in Vietnam to transport heavy cargo and recover crashed aircraft. Better known as the Skycrane, the CH-54 was named after an 18th century chief of the Wyandots in Ohio. Chief Tarhe was said to be tall and slender, prompting the nickname "the Crane."

**Able to lift 10 tons** of payload, the CH-54 and (and its civilian sibling, the S-64) spins a six-bladed rotor 72 feet in diameter. This one appeared at the 1991 air show. The CH-54 faded from military service in the 1990s. Erickson Air-Crane bought the S-64 type certificate from Sikorsky in 1992 and continues to produce and sell the huge aircraft as the S-64.

SKY
CRANE

**Left:** A Bell UH-1 "Huey" lifts troops in a 1985 tactical demonstration. Far right, top: The Army replaced the Vietnam-era Huey with the Sikorsky UH-60 Black Hawk; this one flew in the 1990 air show. By 2007, the Black Hawk was being replaced by the UH-72 Lakota, built by the American Eurocopter division of EADS.

**Right, top, and far right, bottom:** The Air Force CV-22 Osprey made its first appearance at the 2007 air show. Below: The craft that demonstrated tiltrotor technology was Bell Helicopter's XV-15, built for an Army/NASA research program. Bell flew this aircraft, one of only two built, to the 1990 show.

**Right, bottom:** The Army Aviation Heritage Foundation formed its Sky Soldiers Demonstration Team to help the civilian American public connect with the American soldier. The team introduced its four-ship AH-64 Cobra attack helicopter team, painted in Army Recruiting colors, at the 2006 show. It proved to be a successful audition for the Army, which became the team's sponsor.

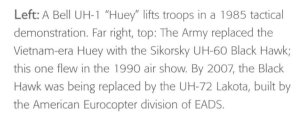

**Far left:** A Marine Corps crew from HMM-162 in Jacksonville, NC, stirred the air of the 1995 air show with the tandem rotors of this Boeing CH-46 Sea Knight. Now VMM-162, the "Golden Eagles" squadron has retired the Sea Knight and transitioned to the MV-22 Osprey.

**Left:** Sky Soldiers Volunteer Jake Allen helped crew the team's UH-1 Huey for media flights at the 2006 air show.

**Below:** Armed with a 30-millimeter cannon, Hellfire missiles and rockets, the Boeing AH-64 Apache is flown by nine countries. This U.S. Army Apache was at the 2007 air show.

# AIR RACERS

Arrayed in rings or rows, the pumping pistons of warbirds converted to race planes excite a crowd. The Dayton Air Show hasn't hosted an air race in recent years, but air racing is a part of the Dayton area's aviation heritage, from the 1924 International Air Races to the jet-age races in the National Aircraft Shows of 1953 and '54. Dayton also hosted Formula V air races in the early 1990s. In more recent years, it has paid homage to air racing with exhibition flights of famous race planes, such as these unlimited-class Reno racers in the 2003 air show—Bob Odegaard in his F2G-1D Super Corsair No. 57 leading Dirk Leeward in his P-51 Mustang Cloud Dancer and former astronaut Hoot Gibson in the red-and-white Hawker Sea Fury Riff Raff.

RACERS

**Left:** Bob Odegaard rescued his red-and-white Goodyear F2G-1D Super Corsair from decades of neglect and restored it to the condition it was in when it won the Tinnerman Trophy in the 1949 Cleveland Air Races. Built to counter Japanese Kamikaze attacks in World War II, the Super Corsair's 28-cylinder engine was rated at 3,500 horsepower for takeoff. The airplane's power and good handling made it a natural for closed-course racing and tight turns around pylons. "It's hard to taxi, but it's nice to fly," Odegaard said in 2001.

**Below and right:** Formula V (pronounced Vee) air racing was created as an affordable category for racers with limited funds. The race planes are restricted in size and power. Dayton hosted Formula V races in 1993, '94 and '95. A green hornet decorated the tail of Butch Mankovich's Hornet's Revenge. Brian Dempsey lavished attention on his plane.

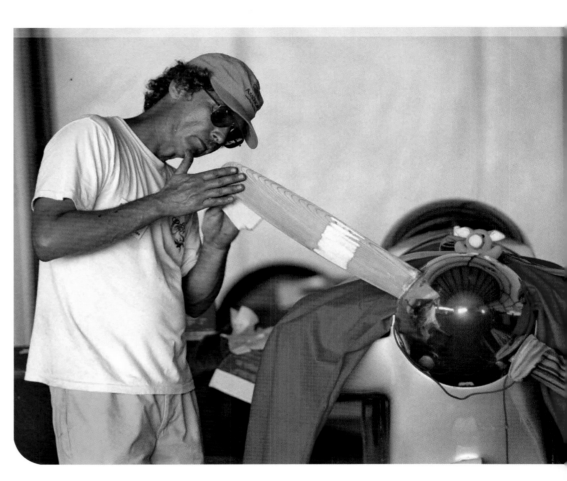

"It's a lot like the Indy 500, only we do it 50 feet off the ground."—Jim Vliet, Formula V air racer, 1995

Homebuilt from plans or kits, Formula V airplanes are smaller and simpler than the big Reno racers. Jim Vliet had little trouble raising the tail of his Sonerai-I so tech inspector Bill Holland could prepare it for weighing, in 1993.

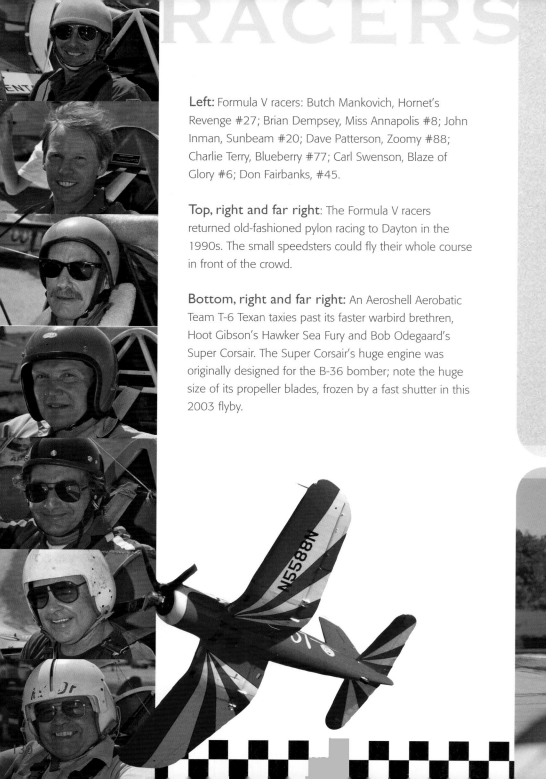

**Left:** Formula V racers: Butch Mankovich, Hornet's Revenge #27; Brian Dempsey, Miss Annapolis #8; John Inman, Sunbeam #20; Dave Patterson, Zoomy #88; Charlie Terry, Blueberry #77; Carl Swenson, Blaze of Glory #6; Don Fairbanks, #45.

**Top, right and far right**: The Formula V racers returned old-fashioned pylon racing to Dayton in the 1990s. The small speedsters could fly their whole course in front of the crowd.

**Bottom, right and far right:** An Aeroshell Aerobatic Team T-6 Texan taxies past its faster warbird brethren, Hoot Gibson's Hawker Sea Fury and Bob Odegaard's Super Corsair. The Super Corsair's huge engine was originally designed for the B-36 bomber; note the huge size of its propeller blades, frozen by a fast shutter in this 2003 flyby.

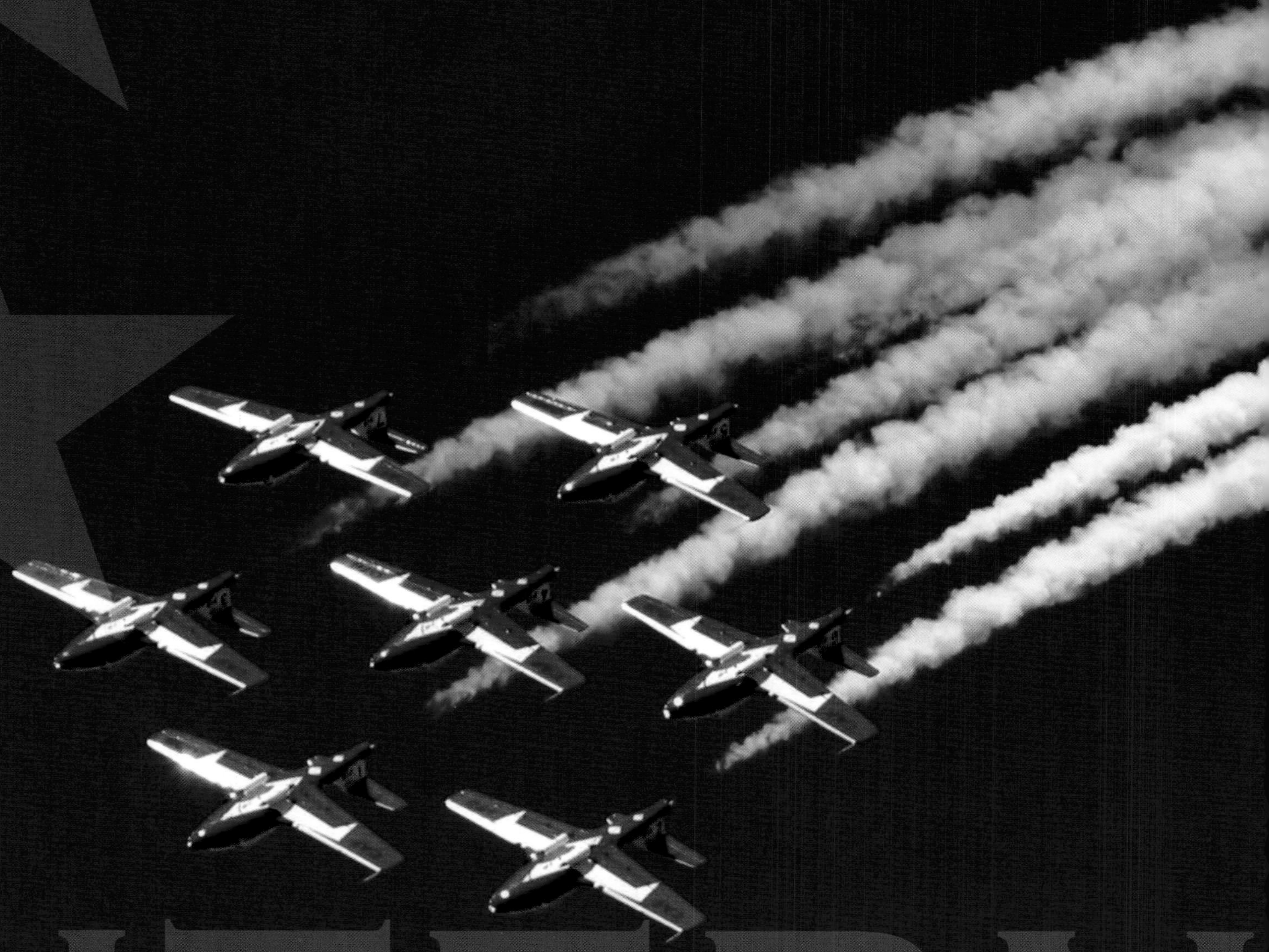

# INTERN

# INTERNATIONAL

From the Canadian Forces' Snowbirds to Cold War adversaries, international participation has been an important element of the Dayton Air Show for decades. Even in the depths of the Cold War, Soviet generals attended the 1953 and '54 National Aircraft Shows. The Brazilian Smoke Squadron has brought its stylish act to several shows, most recently in 2007. Aircraft have come from Britain, Germany and other countries. The most dramatic international presence was a visit by two Soviet MiG-29 fighter jets and their An Il-76 support ship at the 1990 air show. The MiGs shared the static display with America's F-117 Stealth fighter, then still highly classified.

**Left and far right, top:** Wearing borrowed gear, Tim Gaffney made one small step for Glasnost at the 1990 air show by flying in a MiG-29 Fulcrum fighter jet with Valery Menitsky, chief test pilot of the Mikoyan Design Bureau and a Hero of the Soviet Union. Gaffney was one of the first westerners to fly in the frontline Soviet fighter jet. He wasn't alone: then-Lt. Col. (later Maj. Gen.) Ed Mechenbier, commander of the Ohio Air National Guard's 162nd Tactical Fighter Squadron in Springfield, flew the MiG on the same weekend. Such exchanges helped warm relations between the Cold War adversaries. The Soviet Union dissolved at the end of 1991. Menitsky died of cancer in January 2008.

**Top, right and below:** The United Kingdom's Hawker Siddeley (now BAE Systems) Nimrod MR.2 maritime patrol aircraft visited Dayton air shows more than once over the years. British crews sometimes commandeered an air show golf cart. Bottom, right and far right: The Brazilian air force's Esquadrilha da Fumaça—smoke squadron—flew their colorful Tucano trainers to Dayton in 1986, 1993 and 2007.

It was worth waiting out a weekend of bad weather at the 1990 air show for a chance to fly in the Soviet Union's frontline MiG-29 fighter jet. An overcast sky began to clear up just as the show closed, and Menitsky took Gaffney on a short but furious flight to demonstrate the Fulcrum's surprising maneuverability—including a tail slide in the clouds. Menitsky's command of English seemed to fail him when an air traffic controller asked him to visit the tower after he landed.

BLUE A

# BLUE ANGELS

Flying nearly wingtip-to-canopy, four U.S. Navy Blue Angels jets streak by in an echelon formation. The Navy Flight Demonstration Team has been wowing Dayton Air Show crowds with the F/A-18 Hornet since 1989. But the "Blues" have flown at Dayton air shows since at least 1953, when news reports listed the team among the performers at the National Aircraft Show. The team began flying in June 1946 in the propeller-driven Grumman F6F Hellcat. The Blue Angels quickly transitioned to the F8F Bearcat, then into the jet age with the F9F-2 Panther. Later planes included the F9F-5, F9F-8 Cougar, F11F-1 Tiger, McDonnell Douglas F-4J Phantom II and McDonnell Douglas A-4F Skyhawk.

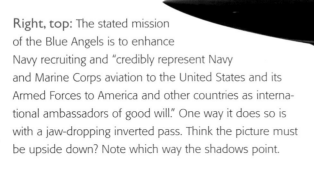

**Right, top:** The stated mission of the Blue Angels is to enhance Navy recruiting and "credibly represent Navy and Marine Corps aviation to the United States and its Armed Forces to America and other countries as international ambassadors of good will." One way it does so is with a jaw-dropping inverted pass. Think the picture must be upside down? Note which way the shadows point.

**Right, bottom:** With no margin for error, the pilots must have absolute trust in their machines, and in the technicians who maintain them.

**Far right, top:** Lt. Cdr. Kevin "Kojak" Davis was the team's announcer in 2006. At the Dayton Air Show that year, he gave Photographer Ty Greenlees a memorable ride in the Number Seven Hornet, a two-seater. Kevin became Number Six, one of the performing pilots, for the 2007 season. He died that year while flying at another air show. We won't forget him.

**The Blue Angels** are based at Naval Air Station Pensacola in Florida, but they do their winter training here at NAF El Centro in California. The region's arid climate and desert terrain give the Blue Angels the sunny weather and remote location they need for training. We visited El Centro in 2006 and found the team just as busy as during the air show season.

Working behind the scenes is a large team of enlisted personnel and officers.

**Left:** AO1 Dawn Hannon was the squadron's first female crew chief. When we met her at El Centro, she summed up the crew chief's vital responsibilities in just a few words: "We take care of the pilot and the jet."

**Below:** Lt. Cdr. Tarah Johnson was the squadron's flight surgeon in 2006. On the remote Shade Tree bombing range (which has neither trees nor shade) she was part of a ground team that monitored the squadron's training flights from a mock announcer's stand.

**The Navy jets** are only a part of the Blue Angels' show. Sharing the stage is Fat Albert Airlines, the Blue Angels' Lockheed Martin C-130T support ship. It's operated by an all-Marine Corps crew of three officers and five enlisted personnel. **Fat Albert's** signature maneuver is its pyrotechnic takeoff, boosted by eight solid-fuel JATO (for Jet-Assisted Take Off) rocket bottles. With all rockets firing simultaneously, Fat Albert climbs out at a 45-degree angle and reaches a thousand feet in fifteen seconds.

The six performing aircraft of the **Blue Angels** join up at the end of a performance. Whenever they fly at the **Dayton Air Show**, they are the closing act —and the one the crowd waits for.

# THUNDERBIRDS

The Thunderbirds are the U.S. Air Force's jet demonstration squadron. Their precision maneuvers showcase the capabilities of modern high-performance aircraft and illustrate the high degree of professional skill required of Air Force pilots. The squadron was activated at Luke Air Force Base in Texas in 1953. Its first major air show, in September of that year, was the National Aircraft Show at Dayton Municipal Airport in Vandalia. The squadron flew Republic F-84G Thunderjets. The unit moved in 1953 from Luke to its current home, Nellis Air Force Base in Nevada. With Wright-Patterson Air Force Base as the region's biggest employer, and a large population of retired Air Force personnel, it's no surprise the Dayton Air Show's most popular act is the Thunderbirds. They typically perform every other year, alternating with the U.S. Navy Blue Angels.

THUND

ERBIRDS

**Left:** The Thunderbirds have flown a succession of front-line fighter jets over the years—the Republic F-84G Thunderjet (1953-54), F-84F Thunderstreak (1955), North American F-100 Super Sabre (1956-1969, with a short stint in the Republic F105B Thunderchief in 1964), and the McDonnell Douglas F-4E Phantom II (1969-1973). In 1974, fuel shortages prompted a switch to the smaller but more economical Northrop T-38A Talon trainer. The squadron returned to fighters with the General Dynamics (now Lockheed Martin) F-16A in 1983 and the "C" model, shown here, in 1992.

**Center:** The knife-edge pass by the opposing solos is always a crowd-thriller. Almost as difficult is snapping a picture in the split-second that the two speeding jets are opposite each other.

**Right:** Silhouetted against a blazing sun, the Thunderbirds join up in a six-ship formation for the maneuvers that conclude their performance.

While the Thunderbirds' six performing pilots get most of the attention, the show wouldn't go on without the squadron's enlisted personnel. Here a ground crew manhandles one of the nine-ton jets into its parking position, precisely in line with the other jets.

**Appearances count**, so Thunderbird crew chiefs keep their jets showroom-clean—even at home on Nellis Air Force Base in Nevada. We visited the Thunderbirds' home base in 1994 and watched this crew chief lavish care on his jet. Of course, keeping the canopy clean isn't just about looks: Good visibility is critical to Thunderbirds pilots flying in tight formations at jet speeds.

**Hot exhaust** from the lead F-16C's engine wrinkles the air in this long-lens shot down the runway. The thunderous chorus of the four formation jets signals the air show's headline act is about to start.

Thunderbirds squadron members emphasize precision on the tarmac as much as in the sky. Here, the ground crews march in formation to show center as the squadron's four-ship diamond formation prepares to launch for another performance. Because of their popularity, the military jet team is the air show's grand finale on both weekend days. When the jets touch down at the end of Sunday's performance, it marks the closing of another Dayton air show—and time to begin anticipating the next one.

# BIOGRAPHIES